Copyright © 2018 by Lauren Ashley Morrison
All rights reserved. This book or any portion thereof
may not be reproduced or used in any manner whatsoever
without the express written permission of the publisher
except for the use of brief quotations in a book review.

Printed in the United States of America
First Printing, 2018

ISBN 978-1-387-53046-5

Publisher: Lulu.com

With any questions about publishing or about the book, please contact the author.

Abundant Marketing
Ashley Morrison
875 Walnut Street – Suite 330
Cary, NC 27511

www.abundantmarketingsm.com

Dedication

To the guiding force that led me to open this business as well as write this book, thank you for all of the opportunities and trials placed in front of me that made me ready for this journey.

To all my clients, thank you for all you have let me learn through your businesses that guided me to the creation of this book.

Contents

1. The Starting Point	7
2. Determining Your Destination	13
3. Driving With Determination	19
4. Driving The Back Roads	28
5. Let's Plan Your Drive	37
6. Clarifying The Route	39
7. Checking For Traffic	42
8. Stay Alert!	45
9. Accidents and Failures	50
10. How Should I Handle Marketing?	53
Appendix	57

Chapter One
The Starting Point

If this book has reached your hands and you don't know who I am, I want to take a moment to introduce myself. My name is Ashley Morrison and I am an entrepreneur who has made my business and my life about helping other business owners. Abundant Marketing is my business and we are helping local businesses grow without breaking the bank!

I believe you'll have a better idea of what you're going to get out of the book and whether this is the right book for you if you know a little bit more about our story first!

Abundant Marketing has been the answer to so many of my prayers. There was a lot that came before Abundant Marketing that led to the creation of the company that exists today.

Where It All Started

I am a little bit of a rare bird around Raleigh, NC... I was born and raised in the area. Even crazier, I've never moved away! You see, Raleigh is so well known for great jobs and great schools that everyone has moved here. But, I am one of the very few individuals my age who has lived here all her life!

After graduating from a local high school in May of 2010, I went on to North Carolina State University and graduated with a degree in Marketing in 2013. If you just did the math on that, you are correct! I gained my college degree in just 3 years. I did so for two reasons:

1. The price of a college degree scared the mess out of me. One meeting with the financial aid office and I was on the fast track.

2. I am a highly motivated self-starter... almost to my disservice.

I had always planned to find a great job where my marketing skills could be put to use after graduating. While I was a senior at NC State, I was working in a local restaurant when I met the owner of an advertising agency who ended up offering me a job! While being a full-time student, I would work in the afternoons at the ad agency then in the restaurant in the evenings. It was a very crazy time in my life.

After college graduation, I was offered a full-time position at that advertising agency. I was still working 8 to 4 every day, but I wasn't making enough to make ends meet. So, I would go to the restaurant every afternoon at 4:30 then work until midnight. It was a little too much for me and I knew there had to be something better.

It led me to ask the question: "Why do I even have a college degree if I have to work this much," and "Who lied to me and said you can make all this money when you come out of college?" On a side note to anybody reading this who is looking for a job in marketing - just because they say you're going to make a certain amount of money a year does not mean it's actually going to happen.

The Lost Year

These questions and the struggles I was facing led me to what I now call my "lost year." All of these questions reminded me of the words of a very wise professor who said, "If you're going to work in marketing, you have to put in at least 10 years in a sales position before you will ever get a marketing position." So, I went back to the career coach at NC State and I asked for help.

During my "lost year", I bounced from job to job very quickly. I was trying to figure out where I fit. I learned a lot of good things, but I also experienced some very negative things.

While I was interviewing for positions during my lost year and asking for marketing positions in smaller companies, I received a lot of valuable feedback. Many said they loved my ideas, but could not afford a full-time marketing person on their staff. In those situations, I would ask if there was such a company that could serve them. Most companies had no idea if there was a company and the few who did know had very nasty answers about the companies out there.

Eventually, I found sales positions in more medium-to large-sized companies. There was one thing that was consistent in all of my sales positions: I was put in front of a computer and a phone and told to get started cold calling for 8 hours a day. As I sat there and tried to convince myself that I could do this for the rest of my life, I just felt like there was a better way to grow a business.

The Best of the Worst

My favorite sales and marketing strategy that I learned from that lost year was gained while I was working for a local company *(I can't name the business because you guys could all go read my LinkedIn profile and figure out what company it was.)*

The company would tell us to cold call until we could make contact with someone in the company, whether they were the decision maker or not. After making contact via phone, they told us to send a postcard. And these weren't just any postcards... They reminded me of something that was made in the 1970's. They were supposed to be funny, but they were moderately offensive. While the postcards seemed a little inappropriate to me, they still made me think.

I thought what if we just sent these postcards ahead of the call so that company's decision maker would know who we were when we called. It seemed that it would make the postcards and the cold calls more effective. So, I went to share my idea with the management team. Man, I really wish someone had told me that was a bad idea and to sit quietly at my desk! Their response was, "This is the way we have always done it and we will continue doing it this way!"

That was the moment that I knew I would never work for someone else. I had too many ideas and I had too much of an entrepreneurial spirit to succeed in other businesses. That is when the idea of Abundant Marketing was born!

The Two Big Visions of Abundant Marketing

I wanted to create marketing services that were affordable for a small business and truly allowed them to grow. But, this was not the only vision that I had for Abundant Marketing. The two main visions that I had were:

1. The Marketing/Operations Roller Coaster: I came up with this term on my own, so don't think it is scientific. This refers to the situation where business owners work very hard on marketing for one to three weeks. Then, it works! Then they have client orders they must fulfill. So, they stop marketing and fulfill all the client orders for that one week. At the end of that week, they have no business and begin to panic. Then, they start marketing again. This cycle is one of the biggest reasons I started my business. The marketing/operations roller coaster not only leads to stress, but many business owners will close their businesses because of the anxiety this causes. I wanted local business owners to have access to great marketing strategies that could be set on a regular schedule without them having to

execute everything, so they could focus on running a great business!

2. Change the Climate of How Employees are Treated: In my "lost year," I had so many positions, supervisors, trainers, and coworkers. I saw people who tolerated their jobs and people who could barely make it through the day. In that year, I was promised things that I never received. I was mistreated, yelled at, told I was stupid, and so much more.

I knew there had to be a better way to treat employees. I wanted employees who love to get up and come to work in the morning instead of waking up with the looming feelings of sadness.

On average, 31% of their waking hours at work. That time should be great and employees should feel like they are contributing and making a difference.

I am frequently asked why my company has the name it does. These two visions are the reason the company has the name it does. I wanted to create something that allows business owners like you and our employees to live an abundant life!

So, What's Next?

As you decide to read this book, I want you to know exactly who we are (Abundant Marketing and I) as well as our perspective. I'm a very authentic person and I love helping small businesses. If this book is something that can help you as a small business owner and truly change how you are marketing your business, then I have reached my goal.

If you are a business owner who is looking for help, then you are in the right place! If you want to learn more about marketing, then you're in the right place! If you want to help out a local business owner or suggest they improve their marketing by dropping off a copy of this book, again, you're in the right place!

Flip to the next chapter and let's get started making an impact on your small business and thus, our local economy too!

Chapter Two
Determining Your Destination

Let's go ahead and get started with your marketing plan! You'll learn quickly that I'm a theme kind of girl. One of the ways that I explain marketing and marketing decisions as compared to taking a road trip. When you're driving a car down the road, everybody's going somewhere different but we all take similar paths. So, for each business, we can use similar marketing tactics even though we all have different destinations and we all have different ways that we're going to reach that destination.

You'll notice in this book that we take that same analogy the entire way through the book. So, let's get started!

Why You Are in Business

You as a business owner got into business for one of two reasons:

1. You saw a product or service that was not offered or could be offered better.

OR

2. You have a passion for something.

People always tell me that the answer is both when I ask them to choose. In many cases, the answer is that it's going to be both but one of the two is the predominant reason you started your business. It's important to know what your primary reason is so we know what your goals are.

Let me give you a couple of examples:
- A good friend of mine, we'll call her Susan, is an advocate for families and individuals who are aging and trying to make the decisions on whether they need a nursing home or if they can live in their home. She does this because she's seen how people have been impacted negatively by the Aging medical system that we have in place. That is a passion-based business.

- Another friend of mine, who happens to be a client, opened a Chiropractic firm that serves crossfit athletes. There are a lot of Chiropractic firms out there that are helping individuals but not many that are focused on making sure athletes can perform at their peak. That is a business offering a better service.

That information allows us to determine what's next for the business. Is the business going to grow very large in order to serve a larger population or is the business going to just be you serving your community?

Determining Goals

The big thing that we really want to take a moment to consider is where you want your business to be in a year, 3 years, 5 years, or 10 years.

If you don't have a business plan, I suggest you create one. It's a great way to think through what your business is going to do and where it's going to go. Whether you have a business plan or not, what I want you to do now is to take a moment and make a plan by filling out the questions below.

When determining goals, I want you to think in the term of one year. If you are looking back at yourself and your business one year from now, where would you want to be? Begin by thinking about it in the broad sense.

A few goals could be:
- Increase Revenue
- Hire More Employees
- Spend More Time at Home with Family
- Take Home More Money

These are just a few examples of goals. Your goals could be vastly different and that's okay.

I want you to do this because it's going to help you in the coming chapters to make decisions in terms of what's next.

Which of the Two Reasons Above Led You to Getting into Business? Either a Vision or a Passion?
_____
_____
_____
_____

Where Do You Want to Be One Year from Now?
_____
_____
_____
_____

Did You Skip It?

Did you write down your answers? I know a few of you just skipped over the questions and just came right to the next spot. I'm going to ask you to go back and take a second and reevaluate that decision. Go back up and fill in the information. It seems like a very futile exercise but it's going to make the next few chapters and the decisions you make in your business so much easier.

Next what we need to do is take time to get to know our numbers. This is where a lot of people have to pause and go back to their books to really see where they are. If you need to do that, take some time before continuing.

Now that you have filled out those questions, what are we going to do with that information?

What Does This Information Mean for Me?

One of my favorite sayings is: "A goal without a plan is simply a wish!" Think about that for a second. Really drink that in. A goal without a plan behind it is just a wish. It's worthless, a waste of your time, and you're never going to reach it.

I know that sounds negative and I hate saying things like that, but realistically some people need to hear that. I want you to walk away from this book with a plan knowing where you are going. I want you to have a direction and know the roads that you are going to take to get to your destination.

Set the Beginning Point

In order to set a goal, we have to know where we are starting in order to know the roads to take. This allows us to make important considerations in your business such as:

- What needs to be changed
- What needs to stop happening
- What needs to start happening

In order to know what needs to change and what direction we are going in, it is important to know where we are. Caution: this

is where the math begins! It's simple math, but very important math. Take a moment and write down where you are at right now.

Setting My Goals!

My Goal: By this time next year, I want more _____
_____.

1. In relation to my goal, I am currently at _____
(this can be hours work/revenue/income, and this should be a number)

2. In one year, I will be at _____ hours/revenue/income

3. Take your answer from the second question and subtract it from the first question. Your answer is: _____

4. Take your answer from question number three and divide it by twelve: _____ This is your monthly goal!

    This may have been a little too much math, so let me give you an example. Let's say I want to increase my revenue by this time next year – that is my goal.

1. In relation to my goal, I am currently at $20,000 in revenue
2. In one year, I will be at $32,000 in revenue.
3. Take the answer from the second question and subtract it from the first question. My answer is: $12,000.
4. Take the answer from question number three and divide it by twelve: $1,000/month in revenue to increase per month.

    Everyone relates to his or her numbers differently. Some individuals see what they need to reach on a monthly basis and their chest hurts. Now, I'm not a medical professional (and you should all thank the Lord for that) but I mean flutters due to stress, not chest tightening. If you feel tightening, call 911! If you feel that the goal is going to be cutting it close and seems a little stressful, circle aggressive below.

But, some individuals see their goal and feel comfortable about it. They feel like they can safely reach the goal with time to spare. If you feel this way, circle mild below.

Mild   Aggressive

Your trip down the road is going to make this book similar to a my-own-adventure book where you now can pick your direction. Every business owner and business will travel a different road and take a different path to get to his or her destination. The next two chapters will go through both mild and aggressive marketing campaigns. If you circled aggressive, read chapter three. If you circled mild, go to chapter four.

If you are interested in both mild and aggressive marketing campaigns, feel free to read both chapters. But remember, this is a sometimes-always-never situation. If you circled aggressive, you must implement an aggressive campaign in order to reach your goal. If you circled mild, you can decide which campaigns you want. The campaigns that you choose will determine the path for your journey. Let's hop in the car and start planning your route.

Chapter Three
Driving with Determination

The aggressive marketing campaigns are like driving 9 mph over the speed limit on the highway. If you go any faster, there is a good chance you will get pulled over by a police officer. Now, I'm not suggesting that anyone reading this breaks any laws or speed limits, but we have all seen the cars that are doing this. They get to their destination faster than expected. This is the concept behind aggressive marketing campaigns, they will get you there faster than most others.

As we get started with the aggressive marketing tactics, there is something crucial to remember. If your numbers led to you needing an aggressive marketing campaign, you must have at least one of these campaigns implemented. You can't choose a handful of mild campaigns and expect them to get you where you want to go.

So, let's get started with what those aggressive tactics are. There are more aggressive campaigns out there than the ones that follow; however, we have found that these are the easiest and fastest campaigns to implement in a small business.

Cold Calling

The first marketing campaign is cold calling. Cold calling is a very broad term, so don't panic, close this book and vow to never open it again because you hate cold calling. Let me let you in on a secret... I HATE cold calling too! It literally makes me feel sad when I do it. But, that doesn't mean it isn't a great marketing campaign.

Cold calls can refer to anything that requires somebody to pick the phone up and make an outbound phone call. A few ways we use them are follow-up calls to people that you met at an event or follow-up calls to somebody who requested more information at a networking event. Cold calling could also be calling about an event for event sponsorships or inviting people to a networking event. It can even be a call to people to see if they are a good referral partner. It could also be the true sense of the word cold calling and introducing your company to somebody over the phone.

At Abundant Marketing, we don't approach cold calls the same way. I think it's a huge disadvantage to any company to just pick up the phone and start blurting what you do to somebody on the other end. Instead, we have some very crafty scripts that we used to get the relationship going before just telling people what we do. Cold calling on average has a three per response rate that means:

- 100 Calls Made leads to three appointments set.
- With a 50% conversion rate, you would get 1.5 new clients.

However, our clients are coming out with different numbers. With our scripts or any well-written script, the 3% response rates shoot up to about 7% which means:

- 100 Calls Made leads to 7 appointments set
- With a 50% conversion rate, you would get 3.5 new clients

My first client was a great example of how cold calling or follow-up calls can be used. The first client I ever took was a local bookstore. We used a letter sent in the mail with a little bit of information to introduce our company and the letter also said to expect a call from me in the next seven days. Upon calling that business owner, I got the appointment booked quickly with this woman and I was shocked! When I arrived at the appointment, she was so astounded that I made the follow-up call because, as she put it, "my competitors don't answer their phones." You'd be so surprised what follow-up calls can do and you'd be really surprised how open people are to talking on the phone!

Direct Mail Campaign

Speaking of direct mail campaigns… Our next campaign is direct mail campaigns. So many business owners think sending letters is outdated and it doesn't work. Because of that, many business owners resort to email marketing. We will talk about email marketing in a moment, but direct mail marketing has a huge leg up on email marketing at this point.

Direct mail marketing is sending something via mail. It could be a letter, handwritten note, postcard or other forms of mail.

Many businesses don't receive much mail anymore;however too much information comes through email. Therefore, getting a letter in the mail, especially if it's hand-written, is very exciting.

You will notice that direct mail campaigns show up on both the aggressive and the mild marketing tactics. This has to do with how the campaign is created. If it is something that you can follow up on (you have a name and phone number,) it is an aggressive campaign. If there is no way to follow up (typical for Every Door Direct Mail campaigns or large mail house campaigns,) then it is a mild marketing campaign.

One of my first big girl jobs was in a direct mail advertising agency. In that agency, we taught our clients that the average response rate for direct mail was one percent. However, since then, it is closer to four percent which means:

- 100 letters sent means four appointments booked
- With a 50% conversion rate, you would estimate two new clients

Direct mail is another marketing tactic that we use around Abundant Marketing. It could be my background that led me to it or it could just be how well I have seen it work for other businesses. We send letters and handwritten notes – depending on the service and client we are trying to reach.

What I love about direct mail, at least the way our letters work, is that business owners get the letter and have the time to read about what we do. They can digest that information and go to our website to learn more about us before we call them.

Paired with the follow-up call, the conversion rate on direct mail jumps tremendously. At Abundant Marketing, when we send our letters, we know that two individuals out of ten will book a meeting. Typically, one will convert into a client.

The Drawback: There is one big drawback though... List creation! Direct mail can be a timely project because you have to build a good, high-quality list in order to get the response rate. Building a list can take a lot of time then folding the letters and stuffing envelopes can take a lot of time too.

Hosting an Event

In the Raleigh area, events are becoming one of the most popular marketing tactics! An event doesn't have to be just a room with you standing in the front preaching to potential clients (please don't do that – no one will ever come back to your events!) An event

could be a networking event, an open house, a social, or a whole lot of other things.

Events can be extremely successful based on the people you get in the room. The majority of the work for event marketing is done ahead of the event. There is plenty of work that goes into inviting the right people and promoting the event. The nice part is, once you're at the event, the event does the work for you.

For example, I hosted a large conference for small business owners in the Fall. I spent a great deal of time working with partners and speakers to plan a great event. We set goals, posted on social media, organized agendas and went out door-to-door marketing the event. When the day came, 67 small business owners were all sitting in one room!

The average response rate of individuals who attend an event and then turn into a client is 13% on average depending on the event the number. What that means is:

- At my 67-person event, you would expect 8.7 individuals to request a meeting (we had 9 requests a meeting)
- From those nine meetings, you would expect 4.5 clients

Events are not only there for B2B businesses, they're also great for medical practices to host. It gives potential patients a chance to come in and learn about how to eat healthier or live healthier lives. It's great for consumer product companies to open their doors and create a less threatening environment.

If there is an easy system in place to put on a regular event with planned aspects, events can be a valuable marketing tool. But, when you have to create a new event every time, the cost may outweigh the benefit.

Email Marketing

So, email marketing... This is one of the most widely used marketing campaigns and probably one of the most annoying campaigns, too! This is another campaign that you'll notice will show up on both the aggressive and mild campaign list for the same reason as direct mail. If you have a concrete list including follow-up information for each individual, then it's aggressive marketing campaign. If it's just an email blast with no phone numbers to follow-up with and you can't track, then that's a mild marketing campaign. It'll even count as mild if you don't have a follow-up plan in place!

Email marketing is something I try to deter most businesses from using. I do so because we have all received email campaigns that we automatically delete. Come on, be honest with me, you have deleted at least one email from a local business today, haven't you? You may not have even opened that email, and if you did, did it really elicit a response from you?

We have to think that way when choosing our marketing campaigns. If you're going to have to compete against 12 other companies that are all trying to get this consumer's attention in their email inbox, how are you going to set yourself apart? Can you really set yourself apart? Before we go any further into email marketing, let's have a look at the numbers:

- An average email has a 20% open rate
- Once opened, there is a two percent click-through rate
- Once they click through, there is a 20% conversion rate

So, let's take that math one step further:
- If you send an email to a list of 1,500 individuals, 240 will open the email
    - From that 240, six individuals will click through
    - From that six, 1.2 individuals will convert into customers

To me, that feels like a lot of waste. An email list of 1,500 individuals could cost upwards of $2,000. I don't mean to be harsh but, those are really bad numbers. And if you're still feeling very enthusiastic about email marketing and thinking it's the way for you to go, we might need to go back to the drawing board for your goals.

Now, I'm not saying all email marketing is bad. I do suggest all companies have an email newsletter to stay engaged with their customers, prospects, and referral partners. But, I try to tell them to take a creative approach. Keep it short, it doesn't need to be too long or people won't read the whole thing.

A newsletter, in particular, is a mild marketing campaign, not an aggressive one; so let's save that for the next chapter...

Networking

Our team LOVES networking! 31% of our business comes from networking so that does make us a little biased. There are a handful of phenomenal networking groups available in all communities. If you personally need some suggestions, take a look at the appendix! There are some great suggestions in there, no matter where you are located.

One of my favorite types of networking is called seat-exclusive networking. There are many organizations that have seat exclusive networking (and I would tell you my favorite, but I don't have the legal right to use its name, so you will just have to guess.)

The first crucial aspect of an effective networking strategy is choosing the group wisely! You want to find a group that could refer business to you or is in a similar industry to your best clients. A few tips I have learned along the way are:

1. *Size doesn't matter.* Don't go for the groups that are the largest, because it doesn't always indicate quality. Most likely, you won't be able to develop more than 5 to 6 good relationships from a networking event. It doesn't matter if there are 20 or 60 networkers in the room – you won't get to all of them anyway.

2. *Not every group is right for everyone.* In our area, there are a lot of women-only groups. That is not a fit for my business, so that is not an event I regularly attend.

3. *Know your goals.* In an open networking events (a large room with a bunch of people standing around,) it's okay to have the goal of closing clients. In a meeting where you can ask for referrals, make your goal gaining a certain number of referrals, not clients from the individuals in the room.

Also, don't be the guy that goes to a networking meeting, grabs everyone's business cards, and add them to your monthly newsletter list. Everybody hates that guy! It's not bad to grab business cards, but then go back to your office and send an email asking people if they'd be interested in setting up a one-on-one. A one-on-one meeting is an opportunity for each of you to learn more about each other's businesses. If you have a one-on-one, before leaving, ask if you can stay in touch monthly through your email newsletter list. That is an appropriate way to do it.

The best part about seat exclusive networking (instead of open networking) is that you meet on a regular basis. In a weekly networking meeting, you tell the members of your group what you're looking for in your business, whether that's a client or referral partner. And you develop relationships with people who are out there looking for your potential clients for you. It creates less work for you and it really develops relationships.

A great example of how seat exclusive networking works well is a team including a mortgage lender, realtor, and insurance professional. If you are in the insurance business, look for a real estate agent or a mortgage lender! These individuals are working with people who are buying and selling their homes and they will know when a new homeowner needs homeowner's insurance.

Depending on the number of referral relationships that you have and the quality of those relationships, you can estimate how much business you can be getting on a regular basis!

So, What's Next?

Those are some of the best aggressive marketing campaigns that I've seen used and I've helped my clients use across all industries. There are different approaches to each campaign depending on each industry, but they all go back to the same basic techniques.

Have you ever seen the popular street racing movie (I can't name the movie because I don't want to get in trouble.) When they are street racing, they push the nitro button to go even faster at the end to win the race. That is like pairing aggressive campaigns with mild campaigns. They will fuel each other and move much more quickly towards the goals.

Aggressive campaigns can pair very well with mild marketing campaigns, so if you're interested, head over and read chapter 4 and learn more about the mild marketing campaigns. If you are not, skip to page 37 and complete the "next steps" activity!

Chapter Four
Driving the Back Roads

We are creating your custom path to your business goals through marketing campaigns. I like to explain a marketing campaign as a journey similar to driving.

The marketing campaigns we choose determine the pace we take towards that goal. Aggressive campaigns are like driving over the speed limit on the highway. When done correctly, you will get there quickly.

Mild campaigns are similar to driving the back, country roads to your destination. It is a much slower and safer approach to growing a business, but not right for someone who is running late. So, let's move into those milder marketing tactics.

If when you set your business growth goals, you felt the pressure was on, an aggressive marketing tactic is necessary. If you felt like your goal was more attainable, then you only need mild marketing campaigns. I always struggled with the sometimes-always-never math questions in geometry and algebra. Unfortunately, this is one of those times you are going to use what you learned in math class:

- If you need an aggressive campaign, you must ALWAYS have an aggressive campaign in place.
- You can NEVER have only a mild campaign or you won't reach your goal.
- If you do not need an aggressive campaign, you can SOMETIMES have an aggressive campaign in place in addition to a mild one. But, be ready for quicker growth than you expected.

I hope that math helped. If not, I'm sorry, math wasn't my strong suit either. The point is, while mild campaigns are still great, they can't be relied upon 100% of the time in order to bring business.

Abundant Marketing started as a social media marketing company for local small businesses. Social media is a mild marketing campaign. When I first started my business, I taught my clients that they were going to need to choose an online and an offline marketing campaign.

Now, I teach that if new business is the goal, there must be an aggressive campaign in play with a mild marketing campaign.

Social Media Marketing

The first mild marketing campaign I always share is the one with which I started my business... social media marketing. Social media is my area of expertise!

The first thing to know about social media is that it must have a strategy to it. It can't simply mean writing posts and putting them up on Facebook - there's so much more to it than that!

The ultimate goal of social media is to get people to your business's website. Your website should be able to give potential clients enough information about your business in order to decide they're the right client for you. It should also tell them if they want to contact you or not. If your website doesn't do that, then social media won't work well for you. The best way to tell if your website is working or not is by the health of the leads the website is developing *(if you are not receiving contact form fill-outs on your website, call us immediately! That's a HUGE problem!*) If you don't have a website, social media typically doesn't work as well.

Social media is also a balancing game. There should be a balance of social media post content. 80% of your posts should be something that is beneficial to your followers and 20% should be promotional. However, many small business owners make 100% of their social media posts promotional. This starts to bother followers and then followers start falling off.

There are a lot of other mistakes that can be made in social media and a lot more strategy that goes into social media. But I don't have the time in this book to write all of that out for you. If you want more information about that, be sure to contact us!

One of my favorite examples of the success seen through social media is a chiropractic firm that I brought on as a client in my first year of business. They were paying a large, national company to run stock posts (you know the ones that every company has in one industry.) They weren't getting anything from social media or their marketing as a whole. We began running Facebook ads and they grew from one office running at three-quarters capacity to two offices running at full capacity.

Now, it's not a good idea to just start a social media strategy on your own, hire a company, or hire an intern just to put post up on social media without a plan. Before asking anybody else to do social media marketing for you or doing it yourself, it's important to make sure there's a strategy behind it. You should know what you hope to gain through social media marketing. Pro Tip: There are ways to make social media aggressive marketing campaign!

Pay-Per-Click Ads

Another common marketing campaign that is pushed towards small businesses is pay-per-click ads.

There are a handful of types of thse ads:
- Google pay-per-click
- YouTube video ads
- Social Media Ads
- Banner Ads

This is one of the most heavily pushed marketing tactics by other marketing companies because it's very easy for a marketing company to monitor numerous accounts due to the software now available.

However, pay-per-click ads are a waiting game. They don't work overnight and typically it takes about 2 to 3 months, depending on the business, to really start to see results. If a small business has the time to wait for pay-per-click ads to work, we love implementing them.

Pay-per-click ads are a really cool tool. Once they are set up, and working correctly, the business can start watching clients flow in. However, not many businesses have the time to wait and, if that is the case, then businesses shouldn't consider pay-per-click ads.

A lot of people ask me what type of pay-per-click ads are best. The answer is 'it depends.' I'm sorry for such a vague answer. Certain businesses and certain industries function in very specific ways. Thus, everyone needs different types of pay-per-click ads.

The clients we have seen with the most success through social media ads are attorneys, specifically a bankruptcy attorney. We target the ads towards individuals who show an interest in credit cards and we use very vivid images of money, credit cards, and debt. What we have seen is that people who are interested in credit cards enough for Facebook to know are great potential clients for a bankruptcy attorney (and very easy for them to convert!)

Email Newsletter Campaigns

Monthly newsletters are the most successful version of an email campaign. I love to teach my clients to do a monthly newsletter! Monthly newsletters work really well for all businesses. Now, some businesses can get away with a higher frequency of a newsletter such as weekly or bi-monthly. But this is very industry specific. For example, a restaurant with weekly specials is much more likely to have clients who are okay with a weekly newsletter than a CPA firm. However, if you are not sure about your business, then go ahead and do once a month.

What I like to teach my customers to do is to partner their monthly email newsletter with other campaigns they're doing at the moment.

- If you're doing a direct mail campaign, send a version of your newsletter to anyone who doesn't respond to the mail campaign. This is a great way to stay in touch with leads that did not follow up with you through the existing campaign you did.

- Another great partner for the monthly newsletter is social media. If you're using social media as one of your campaigns, occasionally post a link where people can sign up to receive regular updates. This allows interested followers to opt into your monthly newsletter list and gain information that could convert them into clients.

I do caution my clients not to use an email newsletter list as a prospecting tool. In other words, don't buy a completely cold list and send your newsletter to them. Cold lists that can be purchased aren't always the best and could end up getting you locked out of your email software account.

PRO TIP: If you send an email newsletter, monitor how many times people open the email. Then, call individuals who open numerous times and ask if you can answer any questions.

I did this in a recent newsletter my team sent out. We called a florist who opened the email 8 times. When we called, we found out she used a marketing company to send postcards for her, but she had no idea who they were sending to or how many were being sent. She just kept paying her invoices! Our email campaign allowed our team to come alongside her, identify how the marketing was being done, and suggest a few campaigns to partner well with what she had going.

Video

Video marketing is something that's gotten a very positive reputation in the last few years. It sounds like video marketing is the end-all-be-all in the marketing world. Now, I'm not saying that it's not. I'm saying that some of the statistics may be a little bit misleading.

The statistics say that videos help convert 80% more individuals on a landing page. But, this is like the purse sales where they say its 90% off of 10% which ends up saving about 20 bucks.
- Landing pages have a 2.35% conversion rate
- Video helps convert 80% more leads
- Landing pages with a video have a 4.23% conversion rate

Out of 100 individuals who land on a landing page, that two versus four individuals converting. When the average cost of a video is $1,500, that doesn't sound great, does it? It only would be if you are selling something that generates more than $775 in revenue per transaction.

In addition, video marketing doesn't do well when not partnered with another campaign. In the example above, the landing page has SEO tactics and probably social media fueling it. When video marketing sits on its own, it has a very low response rate, so low that I would dare to say that video cannot stand on its own as a marketing campaign.

A great example we have seen a client use to get the most out of video marketing is Facebook ads. A local wellness company uploaded promotional videos and ran them as Facebook ads in order to book more coupon requests.

Direct Mail

Another mild marketing campaign is direct mail campaigns done without tracking. An example of a direct mail campaign without tracking is Every Door Direct Mail or EDDM.

Every Door Direct Mail is used by a lot of small businesses because it's the easiest way to get to the largest number of consumers and it is the most accessible. However, it may be a pricier version of direct mail campaigns.

There are large direct mail agencies that are trained in buying high-quality, highly-verified lists that will allow you to track who you're sending it to. Many small business owners don't have the resources to reach out to these companies and thus, they are left with an untrackable mail campaign. And that's okay!

Every Door Direct Mail and Direct Mail campaigns are great to reach out to a large number of people at a very quick pace. However, they do have a small response rate typically about two to three percent.

We have seen direct mail, especially EDDM, work best with companies that bring in a lot of money from one sale. For example, we did a direct mail campaign for a financial advisor that landed him two client meetings. One client is very valuable to him and thus, he will be able to quickly recuperate the cost of his pricey EDDM campaign.

Search Engine Optimization (SEO)

If you are a small business owner, you may have gotten a phone call from an SEO agency in the past. These agencies promise that you'll get to the first page of Google and have the top rank in Google for your industry immediately if you sign up with them. Let me go ahead and promise you something: that's not going to happen! If you get that call hang up.

Search engine optimization (SEO) is something that has to build over time. There is no quick fix and no immediate jump in ranking. So, what is SEO? SEO is building your website and your social media platforms to communicate to the search platforms the way they want to be spoken to. For example, Google likes content-rich websites and they like to see new content added on a regular basis. So, adding regular blog posts to your website is the best way to improve your search ranking and to communicate what your keywords are to the search engines.

Now, blogging is not the only way to improve search engine ranking. It is one of the quickest and fastest ways for a small business to do so.

When deciding if it should go on the mild or aggressive list, the decision was difficult for search engine optimization. I've seen businesses implement SEO tactics and quickly jump to the first page of Google.

I had a client come to me about two years ago and tell me that she needed to be on the first page of Google for her boat rental company. I told her the fastest way to do that was to implement a blogging strategy. Soon after that conversation, we began writing one blog post per week for her and posting them on her website. Within six months, she had ranked over all of her competitors (except for one on one specific keyword.) Even better, she was getting regular phone calls to get her boats rented.

I had another client who owns an electrical company and just wanted to see what SEO could do for her business. We went on an every other week blog post strategy. At one point, we got a little behind on posting due to a holiday. We ended up posting about three blogs to their website all within one week just to get them caught up. This led to the company getting six potential clients to ask for quotes on their website that week.

I don't tell you this so you think that your business is going to get the same thing because we can't guarantee that. I say this because it's been so successful, and it could be for your business, too! This is a great, general overview of some of the mild marketing campaigns.

Chapter Five
Let's Plan Your Drive

So, now what? Did some of these campaigns sound like a ton of fun for you to try? Did some of the campaigns make you feel like you do when you are driving a convertible with the top down on a sunny day? If not, that's okay. It could just be because you don't love marketing as much as I do.

The next step to improving your business and growing your business is to get some of these campaigns going. In the area below, list your two favorite aggressive marketing campaigns and your two favorite mild marketing campaigns (if you only want to try one, only fill in one area:)

Aggressive

_____
_____
_____
_____

Mild

_____
_____
_____
_____

It is extremely important to consider how the campaigns are going to interact with each other. Write out a little bit about how you are going to implement the campaigns and how or if they will overlap:

___
___
___
___
___
___
___
___

Now, if you had absolutely no idea how to fill out the information above – that's okay! It is time to call-in the reinforcements! Our team offers a free 30-minute strategy session to help answer the above questions. Give our fantastic team a call at 919-379-5790 ext. 700 to set up a time now!

Chapter Six
Clarifying the Route

Before ever starting a marketing campaign, it is critical to know who you should be marketing to. It's like getting in a car to drive somewhere with no destination. This is one of the most commonly overlooked aspects of owning and growing a business. This is one thing that I try to help business owners communicate very clearly.

I was doing a workshop recently and I asked a direct sales representative who was her best target client. She responded, "Anyone with a face really." This answer is the equivalent of getting in the car without contacts when you need contacts or glasses. It can be EXTREMELY dangerous or even deadly for your business.

Let me back up just a second. If someone is sitting in front of you asking what type of client they can send to you, be as clear as you possibly can. Even ask for names if possible. Don't give them something so big that they are now checking out of the conversation.

The even bigger problem was, she had no idea to whom she was supposed to market her business. Let me give you a better example of how to answer this question. I helped a local chiropractor develop his target audience to determine the two specific audiences below:

Audience # 1: Chronic Pain
Anyone who is dealing with chronic back, knee, shoulder, or neck pain.
Target Areas: 8 to 10 miles around the office
Interests: Pain Relief and Pain Relief Medications

Audience # 2: Preventing Pain
People, but typically athletes, who are using their joints and muscles on a regular basis and who don't want an injury
Target Areas: 8 to 10 miles around their office
Interests: Running, Swimming, Biking, etc.

These are two examples of a much more highly-defined target audiences. These could still stand to use a little more detail. Not only is this much easier to create a marketing campaign around, but if someone asks you what types of clients you are looking for, these are much more likely to bring a name to the front of mind.

Let's take a moment and help you determine the same information for your business. If you are in a business where you can sell multiple products to multiple target audiences, pick the one best target audience for you. Now, start by answering the questions below:

1. Why Would Someone Use Your Product/Service?
_____
_____
_____

2. Who Would Use This Product/Service?
_____
_____

3. Who Are Your Last 3 Customers? _____
_____

4. When Does the Customer Need Your Product or Service Most?

_____
_____

5. Where Are the Best Places to Meet Your Customers?

_____
_____

6. In what age ranges do your potential clients fall?

_____

7. What kind of jobs/responsibilities/concerns do they have?

_____
_____

8. What product do they need?

_____
_____

9. What makes you the perfect person to offer it to them?

_____
_____

These questions, if answered honestly, can really help determine who your best potential customer is. Take a moment and write out a brief description of one or two of your best potential customers below:

My Best Potential Customer Is:_____
_____
_____
_____

Chapter Seven
Checking for Traffic

Now, it's time to get started! You know what your goals are, you know what campaigns you need, you know who your best target client is. Your journey is outlined and now, it's time to get started. If this is a new marketing campaign that you have never tried before, how will you know the campaign will succeed? How can you know if it will get you what you need?

The simple answer to that is there is no way to know for sure. But, for a completely new marketing campaign, there are a few ways to gain ideas on how it will perform ahead of time.

What Is Marketing Research?

Marketing research is like double checking the traffic before you leave to ensure you will make it on time. The best way to explain marketing research is asking questions before doing something. Marketing research can be done on a handful of levels which typically leads business owners to think they can't do marketing research for their campaigns. But, that's not true.

It is true that marketing research may not be 100% predictive of the results of a potential campaign. It definitely won't be clear enough that you can publish your results in a journal with statistics behind it, but it can give some ideas for tweaks to make before starting.

Who Should I Ask?

We just determined who your best target clients are, start by asking them! If you already have them as trusted clients, start there. If not, create an online survey to send out to individuals in your target audience. Pro Tip: This is a great way to pick up potential clients, especially if they engage in the survey!

What Should I Ask?

The biggest thing I learned when it comes to marketing research is to ask clear, non-leading questions. For example, "Rank your five favorite bowls of cereal from the list below" versus "Are Cheerios your favorite cereal?" The second question leads to an answer and gives the individual answering the survey an idea of how they should answer. The first question will give clear information with much more data.

Another example would be, "How Much Do You Spend versus how much do you budget on vacations? Share a percentage below" instead of "How much do you plan to spend on vacations annually?" and "How much do you spend on vacations annually?" The first question I wrote, and I don't even know where to start with answering it. Whereas, the second questions can be split apart, so the respondent will know exactly what information to share in each area.

A few good questions to ask in relation to a marketing campaign are:
- What are the top 3 ways you would have responded to this campaign?
- What would make you more likely to engage with the campaign?
- What would you change about the campaign?

Many of our clients choose not to troubleshoot marketing campaigns ahead of time because we have seen so many campaigns work in similar businesses. Our Abundant Marketing campaigns are typically our newest material, so we troubleshoot regularly. Because I dream up the campaigns very quickly and put them into play very quickly, I have one or two trusted advisors I ask ahead of time. Then I ask three to five business owners I meet at networking events. Based on the information I receive, I make the decision on whether or not to move forward.

Remember, you can ask your target audience, but also colleagues and family or friends as well. Remember that the data from your target audience will always be better, but that doesn't mean you won't get valuable information (or have a grammar lover catch a mistake) with either group.

Word to the wise. There is a condition called paralysis of analysis. This is where you spend so much time trying to determine how your campaign will work out that you never start. Another great way to explain this is when you wait so long checking traffic that traffic builds while you are waiting, and you are late.

Chapter Eight
Stay Alert!

As we get started with a marketing campaign, it's crucial to monitor the progress on the route. If your destination is 30-minutes away and you've driven for over 20 minutes without making it two-thirds of the way there, we have a problem. Tracking will help you to see this occurring or ensure you are going to arrive on time.

Every marketing campaign should be tracked and followed up on. Thus, if a campaign isn't tracked, it can't be followed up on. There are a few individuals who have told me they are tracking campaigns and, when I ask them how, I find out they aren't actually tracking at all.

A few of their methods have been:
- Post-its on a desk
- The sent email folder
- Called and told a friend

We have a company dog, his name is Yogi (no, don't panic, he doesn't live at the office or belong to Abundant Marketing. He's more like a team member.) However, our team member/office dog Yogi is a rescue. Yogi came home from rescue with a deathly fear of paper. As his owners, we started to try everything to find a way to ease this fear for him. One of the main ways to train a fear out of a dog is desensitization or exposing him to it until it doesn't scare him. We tried this with Yogi and had some odd successes. We found out that he LOVES Post-its! It must be something about the taste of glue on the back. Either way, we now give him post-its to run around within the office when he does something good.

This has backfired on us from time-to-time. The most memorable one is when we were putting an Ikea purchase order together for a new office space... on a Post-it! Yogi got so excited that the Post-it was for him, that he ran across the room, leaped towards the Post-it, and grabbed it right out of my hands.

This odd story is meant to warn you (and scare you a little bit.) If you are tracking your marketing campaigns with Post-its, I will personally send Yogi over to your office and then we will see how good your tracking is afterward! Moral of the story, Post-its are not an acceptable form of tracking!

Great Ways to Track

Tracking all comes down to the specific business. But, I suggest using a method of tracking that is easily accessible from every device because you will never know when you need it. Depending on the number of employees who have to review the information, choose something that is easy to learn or adapt to.

I have regularly been told by my staff, bookkeeper, husband, and many more people that my spreadsheets are way too difficult to understand. So, around our offices, we track our marketing campaigns and follow-up information using a software called Insightly.

A few other really great options for tracking are:
- Spreadsheets – Specifically Google Spreadsheets where you can see them wherever you are.
- Google Documents
- Evernote
- Customer Relationship Management (CRM) Software such as Insightly, Salesforce, Zoho, and many more.
- Project Management Software such as Asana.

There is no right answer on what to use as long as **something** is being used!

How to Follow Up

Now that we have a plan on how to track the marketing campaign, what are we supposed to do with that tracking? Great question… you are supposed to follow up on it and make sales from it!

There are so many great ways to follow up on a marketing campaigns, but my favorite by far is calling. You could also email, walk into the business or a handful of other things. But, I have seen a good, old-fashioned phone call really goes the furthest.

I can't tell you how many clients I have gained because "my competitors never pick up the phone and call." This has become so true that we have added this as a constant service level in our company, too!

Many business owners say that would much rather just send an email. I typically get one response from 100 follow-up emails I send responded to. But, when I call, I typically get four to six responses and about two meetings booked. Now, those are just my statistics, but why waste your time?

Consumer-Based Businesses

For a consumer-based business, you can still follow up with

a phone call. You just have to use some creative ways to find the information. While phone calls are great, answering how you found your target client's information isn't always great. So, consider sticking with the way you initially communicated with the individual. For example, if he reaches out on Facebook, send him a Facebook message.

Follow Up Frequency

The key to following up is frequency. It typically takes seven to eight touches to convert a potential lead. A touch is considered any way that you reach out to a potential client. Your initial campaign will count as a touch.

So, if you stop after one or two touches, you haven't gotten anywhere near close enough to converting leads into clients.

How We Do It

Around Abundant Marketing, we have a 7-touch campaign. It includes the following touches:

1. **Cold Call** – Use an initial call into the business and gain more information about the business.
2. **Send a Letter** – This is a two-page, printed letter that introduces them to us, our services, and our clients.
3. **Follow Up Call** – We call to make sure they received the letter.
4. **Follow Up Email** – We email to make sure they got our voicemail.
5. **Event Invite** – We send a postcard or handwritten note about an upcoming event.
6. **Email Event Invite** – We email a link to attend the event.
7. **Text Message** – We send them a text message asking if they received any of our correspondence.
    a. **Social Media Request** – If the company doesn't have a textable phone number, we request the right contact within the company on LinkedIn or Facebook.

This is just an example, not a guideline. We have added touches and removed touches, but the pattern and the frequency stay the same.

When I speak to large groups, the first question I am asked after sharing this is how close together each individual touch should be. That is another factor that needs to be determined based on the business and the industry. In our industry, the timeline goes as follows:

1. **Cold Call** – Day 1 of the Campaign
2. **Send a Letter** – Day 2 of the Campaign
3. **Follow Up Call** – Day 7 of the Campaign (Enough time for the letter to arrive.)
4. **Follow Up Email** – Day 7 of the Campaign – Typically in the Evening Hours.
5. **Event Invite** – Day 10 of the Campaign
6. **Email Event Invite** – Day 16 or 17 of the Campaign
7. **Text Message** – Day 19 or 20 of the Campaign

As you can see, many of the mild and aggressive campaigns can be used as a touch within your follow-up strategy. That is why I encourage business owners to think about all of them, what they like, and what they are comfortable with.

Our sample campaign above is very effective and like driving 100-mph in a 70-mph zone when fully executed. This can lead me and my team to 5 meetings per week on average and about 2 new clients per week. If you aren't ready for that amount of work in your business, then be careful with this type of campaign or the high follow-up frequency.

I know what you are thinking… this all sounds great, but

marketing doesn't work like this in my business. These campaigns will never work. Well, if you believe this or have experienced it in the past, flip to the next chapter and let's work through that.

Chapter Nine
Accidents and Failures

It happens to the best of us. We plan a campaign, build a great list, execute the campaign perfectly and it fails. It's like when you get in a car accident during your commute. If this has happened to you or is happening to you, don't get discouraged! There could be a few key things that went wrong:

1. Time and Date of Sending: Sometimes there are circumstances outside of our control. Time and Date is something that can be planned for in most circumstances. For example, in the automotive industry, you never call/mail/etc. between the 29th and 1st of any month because they are doing end of the month because they are pushing sales the last few days and reconciling the previous month their first few days.

    a. What to Change: In the future, do more research on your industry and see if the day or time impacted the response of the campaign. Find out when potential clients are engaging with businesses the most and aim for those days and times.

    b. Caution: Sometimes, big current events unravel a marketing campaign (and sometimes, build up a marketing campaign.) For example, when a local Raleigh girl was kidnapped from RDU airport. Many people were online sharing the news story and trying to find her that led to an increased amount of time individuals were online that week. Thus, all pay-per-click ads did tremendously better that week.

2. Method of Delivery: Whenever I speak and share about how ineffective email marketing can be, one business owner always looks at me and tells me how wrong I am. When other business owners in the room see the one business owner that does that, they all share how much they hate email and that they won't open them. But, that doesn't stop anyone from trying.

    a. What to Change: Try the same campaign with a different method of delivery. Try sending a letter or leaving a note at your potential client's door instead of emailing.

3. Number of Touches: I know we just hit on this in the last chapter, but getting the right number of touches is one of the hardest things to do. Trust me, I manage a team of sales professionals and even they don't hit the mark every time. We have a team of cold callers to stand behind them in case they get too busy to make their follow up calls and additional touches.

    a. What to Change: Maybe you need extra help, either from a marketing company (we would be honored to help) or hire a part-time employee to help out.

4. Target Audience: It could be that the target audience was just a little off or the message did not resonate with them.

    a. What to Change: Go back and do a little more marketing research with your target audience. Review the information you receive and take their critiques very seriously.

There is a chance that you did everything perfectly on your

campaign and it still failed. Trust me, it happens occasionally. In this case, it is time to go back to the drawing board and try something different.

If you really want more information on why it failed or want to learn how to choose the right campaign next time, reach out to a marketing consultant for help! But, that is a tough decision, too. How do you know when to do your own marketing? Or hire an intern? Or choose a marketing company?

Let's delve into that decision...

Chapter Ten
How Should I Handle Marketing?

This is a critical chapter if you are a small business owner. Too many small business owners fail because they try to hold on to their money instead of hiring a marketing company and they just can't do it all.

It is equally terrible when a small business goes out of business because its expenses are too high. This is something we do our best to ensure is not happening to our clients. How is anyone supposed to know what they can afford?

Profit First

The profit first theory has impacted my business in profound ways and we try to share it with as many business owners as we can. Profit first was created by a great author (who I aspire to be as good as,) Mike Michalowicz.

The idea is that we all see our business finances as this:

>Revenue
>-Expenses
>---------------
>Profit

But, the way we should really be seeing it is as:

>Revenue
>-Profit
>---------------
>Expenses

This idea teaches us, as business owners, to control our expenses in order to preserve our profits. Our profits are supposed to go towards the reasons that we got into business for ourselves in the first place. Things like nice vacation, less personal debt, more family experiences, etc.

In Mike's book, *Profit First*, he teaches the right percentages for each area of expenses and profits that our businesses should have at each point in business. It teaches how to determine what expenses fall into those areas. I have given an image of his table of distributions below.

	A	B	C	D	E	F
Real Revenue Range	$0 - $250K	$250K - $500K	$500K - $1M	$1M - $5M	$5M - $10M	$10M - $50M
Real Revenue	100%	100%	100%	100%	100%	100%
Profit	5%	10%	15%	10%	15%	20%
Owner's Pay	50%	35%	20%	10%	5%	0%
Tax	15%	15%	15%	15%	15%	15%
Operating Expense	30%	40%	50%	65%	65%	65%

Take a moment and review your finances. Follow the suggestions on the next page and determine what your finance distribution should be.

If you have a lot of questions or if this is an area you struggle with or want more help with, I would really suggest buying Mike's book. Again, it has had a profound impact on my business and I would love to see it do the same for you!

If you looked at the table above, you should now know how much you should be spending on monthly expenses. Is your amount higher or lower than that? That number determines how you will execute your marketing:

The Number You Spend on Expenses is Higher Than It Should Be

Welcome to the DIY marketing section. If your expenses are too high, you either need to cut out some expenses or find a way to do your marketing on your own for now. There are plenty of webinars and local events to attend to get more ideas and tips on how to get started.

Our team sends out of a monthly newsletter with a marketing campaign to focus on for each month, that could be a great place to start! Visit our website to read our newsletter tips and subscribe to the upcoming newsletter.

The Number You Spend on Expenses is Lower Than It Should Be

This is a sign that it is time to start marketing more aggressively and regularly. Many businesses begin seeing success with marketing in about two to three months, so a regular marketing campaign is great for business! There is more than one way to accomplish this, depending on the amount of time and how you feel about other people. Be honest when making this decision:

You Have Extra Time and You Love People

You are a rare breed! And that's ok! If both truly describe

you, then you should hire an intern or employee to train to do your marketing the way you like.

The advantage of this is that the employee is solely your employee and will be trained exactly the way you want him or her to operate. The problems could be:
- You could train him or her the way you want, invest all that time, and he or she could leave the next day.
- He or she may not have all the knowledge or skills you need and you may not be able to train that.
- He or she could have normal employee problems (a lot of time wasting, misuse of time, etc.)

Included in this category is hiring a family member or friend. If you are ready to train him or her on exactly what you need and exactly how to do it, it may work out. But, in over 80% of these scenarios, the business suffers and so does the relationship with the individual.

You Have Extra Time But, You Don't Like People or You Want an Expert

The best solution for most small businesses is hiring someone that already understands marketing and marketing specifically for small businesses. Many individuals hire a family member or someone who did marketing in a large corporation, but that person doesn't understand how marketing tactics need to be adapted for a small business.

Our team would love nothing more than to assist your business! The first time we meet with any business, we ask a few simple questions to learn more about what is going on in the business and give suggestions on what we would do to market that business. Every business owner gets this information whether he or she is going to work with us or not.

Hopefully, this book has allowed you to make some decisions on how you are going to market your business and start growing. Hopefully, you have a path for the journey to reach your business goals. We have added an appendix at the end to help you find networking events.

From the bottom of my heart, I want to thank you so much for taking the time to read this book and I wish you the best in all of your business endeavors!

Appendix A
Great Networking Events in Your Area

Our team, in general, is a big fan of BNI (Business Networking International) networking events. To find your local BNI chapter you can visit, visit this website: _____.

More Networking Events We Suggest for Your Area Are:
-

-

-

Do you want to come with us to one of these networking events? Give us a call at 919-379-5790 ext. 700 and let us know!